The Ultimate Guide Raising Mixed Race Kids

J. Lindt

The Ultimate Guide
Raising Mixed Race Kids

Copyright © 2024 Lindt Publishing

Paperback ISBN: 978-87-975530-0-8

Contents

Introduction

"In diversity, there is beauty and there is strength." — Maya Angelou.

New additions to our families bring us joy. They bring happy tears to our eyes when we see how much they resemble us in their mannerisms, culture and traits. In their identities, we see our own. In their eyes, we see our cultures. And, as they grow and develop, we want them to remain in touch with the cultural identities that make them unique, while being prepared for challenges they undoubtedly will face as they grow up.

Raising children is not easy. Raising multiracial children might be taking it to another level. It involves supporting them as they learn about their cultures and races. Yes, part of this journey is teaching your child how to speak two or more languages, but there is more to it than that. It requires cultivating both their physical presence and internal self-awareness. As the world shrinks into a global village, with people constantly moving across borders, more multiracial children are finding themselves in new, often challenging, environments. Here, their self-esteem is tested. Many children who live where they may not look, dress, worship, or celebrate milestones the way most of their neighbors do struggle with self-esteem issues.

As your multiracial child grows, they may experience hurtful comments about their identity. As they get older, they may have plenty of questions about who they are. As they attend school, they might even struggle to adjust to the culture and educational environment they grow up in. These challenges may make you wonder if there is a blueprint for raising enlightened children who are prepared for the complex challenges they may face. What are the correct parenting techniques? What actions should we take to help our children over-come racial difficulties, and self-esteem issues and to ensure they feel they truly belong to their community?

Key Areas of Focus

Welcome to your new ultimate guide to raising rounded and grounded multiracial children.

- As a parent of a multiracial child, have you ever felt unsure about how to navigate the complexities of their unique identity?
- Do you worry about the challenges they might face in a world that often misunderstands and misrepresents their heritage?
- Are you searching for the tools to equip your child with the confidence and resilience to flourish as a proud and empowered individual?

This book is for you if you answered yes to any of the questions above. In this book, you will learn how to nurture your child's cultural identity and foster inclusive, diverse relationships.

This comprehensive guide helps you navigate through the key areas in easy-to-follow steps:

- Groundwork on how you can best prep yourself and your child
- Practical things you can do to promote cultural diversity
- How to overcome challenges your children might be facing
- How to overcome challenges you, as parents, might be facing

This guide aims to support you through challenges so you can embrace the joy of being a parent to a multiracial child. We focus on the best strategies while avoiding the psychological and historical denseness that makes many books heavy and time-consuming to read. We compiled the essential nuggets of wisdom we learned from our own experiences and gathered the most useful methods you can use to raise your children with mixed heritages.

We all want to be proud parents of children whose traits and cultural uniqueness, confidence and happiness, well-being and self-assuredness shine through, no matter their background. In this day and age, when having a mixed-race identity is often seen as a problem to figure out, I invite you to take a stand and recognize the extraordinary capability of your kids. As multiracial children bravely step outside the boundaries of traditional cultures, they lead the way to a new and exciting future. Possessing the knowledge of two distinct cultures, the skills of multiple languages, and a variety of opinions, they stand on the frontier of tomorrow.

As parents, it's our duty to arm them with the tools to handle hurtful experiences around race, while helping them to build their confidence, self-esteem, competence and a sense of belonging. That is what I offer you in this book.

Why This Book?

Why should you listen to what I have to say? The answer lies in my commitment to change perspectives and provide support where I can. I am not here to claim absolute knowledge or offer one-size-fits-all solutions. Instead, I present you with the culmination of my research, experiences, and dedication to helping and supporting these young minds.

Driving and motivating the creation of The Ultimate Guide: *Raising Mixed Race Kids* are my personal experiences of raising a multiracial child. My wife and I are proud parents of Thai and Danish heritage, and nothing gives us more happiness than our multiracial son. When we moved our family from Thailand to Denmark, we experienced a complete cultural shift. While Thai customs, traditions, and history remained important to us, we of course sought to accept, understand and embrace every cultural element Denmark offered – elements that we would see mixed in our child.

Our experience encompasses the struggle of embracing multiple languages and learning a new language to instill in our son the essence of his Danish roots. We had to find many answers to solutions to challenges like educating our child about race early on, and navigating racial bias and prejudice.

Part of our challenges as parents was the desire to maintain both languages of our unique heritages, which goes beyond learning new words, phrases, idioms and expressions. We wanted to maintain Thai and Danish linguistic nuances to help our son maintain his roots, and understanding the importance of our culture, we embraced every challenge this brought our way. We then tried different approaches to find the right fit for our family and situation.

In this ultimate guide, we bring what we've learned to you, supporting and helping you with what you might be going through as a parent of a multiracial child. We want to help you navigate this challenge with confidence. Our goal is to ensure that when your child begins to grow, they are aware of their heritage and culture, and are happy and confident in who they are and who they have become.

As your child encounters questions about their identity and faces societal challenges, this book will provide you with the essential tools to help them manage these situations with grace and resilience. By learning to embrace and celebrate their heritage, your child can develop a robust sense of self and profound confidence in their personal journey.

We want to guide you every step of the way, ensuring that your child not only recognizes the richness of their heritage but also feels secure and valued for the unique individual they are. We want to inspire support for a generation of children who are not just comfortable in their own skin but also capable of changing the world around them for the better.

Let's get started!

CHAPTER 1

The Groundwork

"We may have different religions, different languages, different colored skin, but we all belong to one human race." — Kofi Annan

Our world is diverse and filled with different cultures and ethnicities, but it's not as simple as bringing people together under the umbrella of humanity and race. We cannot ignore the complexities of multiracial communities and their adverse effects on children as they struggle with their sense of identity. Denying these complexities can leave them feeling lost and alienated in their own families and communities.

In a world where people would turn a blind eye to the impact of racial discrimination, how can we support our multiracial kids to embrace their identities and thrive in the midst of discrimination and prejudice? How can we help these kids flourish when faced with difficult situations related to race and skin color? And how do we better understand the challenges of being a multiracial child?

You might be surprised to learn that a lot of teachers rely on something called the "color-blind theory" when teaching kids in the initial stages of development. This approach has been around for ages, where educators and caretakers assume that young children are incapable of comprehending racial diversity and issues related to race due to their young age.[1] By choosing this approach, they fail to acknowledge and address the real and present influences of race and ethnicity in a child's life. Parents sometimes adopt this approach too. They assume that avoiding the topic of race or multiracial identity is the best way to help their child fit in. We sometimes feel that silencing the topic can perhaps shield our children from experiencing identity confusion and even racism. The thing is, pretending that racism doesn't exist or staying silent about it doesn't protect children from identity confusion or racism. In fact, it can even harm a multiracial child's sense of self. We need to recognize that children can, and do, experience the world in terms of race, and ignoring this fact does them a disservice.

As parents, it is important to acknowledge our children's cultural and racial uniqueness but it's equally important to recognize the stereotypical chains that hold the concept of unity hostage. By moving away from the "color-blind" theory and embracing a more proactive and inclusive educational approach, parents and other caregivers can better support the development of positive racial identities and the cultivation of a genuinely equitable society.

Groundwork #1: Understand Why Celebrating Multiculturalism is Important for Children.

Exploring cultural diversity from your child's perspective offers significant benefits not only for your child but also for you and their peers. Helping your child appreciate their unique identity begins with celebrating multiculturalism. This technique effectively counters the shortcomings of the color blindness theory, which many studies have shown can lead to greater racial issues.

By embracing and celebrating cultural differences, we foster an environment where diversity is seen as a strength and everyone feels valued and respected. This approach not only enriches children's lives but also helps to build a more inclusive and understanding society, laying the foundation for a future where equality and mutual respect are the norms.

Groundwork #2: Embrace Uniqueness

Studies have shown that multiracial children face a higher risk of developing issues like racial misidentification, low self-esteem, violence, substance abuse, and feeling marginalized in two cultures.[2] This makes embracing their uniqueness more important now than ever, helping your child to adjust to their unique characteristics. As parents, we often forget that our children grow in the reflection of who we are and how we act; they absorb our emotions and actions.

You may feel like you do not belong anywhere, given your diverse family background, but you hide it from everyone. However, you should know that people often reject things they do not understand or appreciate. Therefore, the duty of appreciating and celebrating our uniqueness—and that of our children—rests with us.

Every person has unique qualities, strengths, and characteristics that make them who they are. Embracing and accepting these aspects can be a transformative journey of self-discovery and growth. It often involves understanding and appreciating oneself, acknowledging strengths and areas for improvement, and developing a sense of self-worth and confidence.

Having lived in Asia for a number of years, I have experienced firsthand the multitude of races and mix of races in the various countries I have lived in. I have also experienced the racial prejudices that exist, and being Caucasian, I feel like I have gained unique insights from the perspective of being the "other." This experience has enriched my understanding of racial and cultural differences. The multiracial struggle and racism is omnipresent in Asia and I know the situation is very similar in both the EU and America, as immigration and racial blending is a fact of life.

As a parent of a multiracial child, I wanted to raise my child to embrace their uniqueness and feel a strong sense of belonging. I wanted my child to be proud of his mixed heritage and the combination of cultures that flow in his veins. I find that society does not discuss the issue of mixed race enough, so I realized the importance of openly discussing our unique background and highlighting the importance of embracing diversity and celebrating all aspects of our heritage. I encouraged my child to ask questions, explore his own identity, and be proud of who he is.

Over time, my child grew in self-confidence and appreciated his uniqueness. Together, we embraced cultural traditions, celebrated festivals from both sides of our family, and surrounded ourselves with a diverse community that honored and respected our heritage. So, it's important for you as a parent to share your story with your child so they can relate to you and their culture. This helps them feel connected and not alone or alienated in their community or other communities.

One of the best things I implemented in my family life was active discussion. It changed the narrative in my house, especially when it came to racial identity. As parents, we are often so lost in the struggles of life that we forget all of what we do is for our children and their comfort. We place communication with our children aside and miss the opportunity to share potential tips to help them live a balanced life. The busier we get, the wider the gap becomes. As busy as life gets, we must not sideline our children's need for communication and understanding. The conversations we foster can significantly impact their well-being and identity.

Groundwork #3: Eliminate The Stereotypes

Did you know that a 6-month-old child can recognize racial differences? Research from the 90s shows that 6-month-old babies can notice and sort people based on race and physical traits. By ages 2-3, children can identify racial categories, and can form biases as early as 3-5 years, often independently of their parents' views. This highlights the urgency for parents to begin these crucial conversations early, helping their children forge strong, confident identities amidst a diverse world.

Research has consistently shown the importance of engaging children in discussions about race and stereotypes from an early age. Experts warn that avoiding these conversations may inadvertently suggest that racial differences are negative or undesirable. Yet, not many parents are comfortable addressing these topics with their children, and they often delay the conversation until the child is around five years old. However, this may be a little bit late as biases can form much earlier.[3]

To address this, parents need to proactively initiate conversations around race with their children, asking them what they have heard or learned about this issue. By doing so, parents can help dispel any misconceptions or myths that children may have encountered.

It is also important to explain the concept of stereotypes, which are simplified and generalized beliefs or images about a person or group based on certain characteristics they share. Stereotypes are harmful as they disregard the unique qualities of individuals within a particular group. Therefore, as your children grow, you must be committed to exposing them to the diversity in society and educating them about different racial and cultural backgrounds.[4]

Groundwork #4: Understand Racism

In today's increasingly interconnected world, it is of utmost importance for parents to engage in open and honest discussions about racism with their children. Educating children about racism, its impact on communities, and efforts to combat it teaches them to be empathetic and compassionate.

It is essential to acknowledge that racism exists and affects people differently, especially based on the color of their skin. Children with different skin colors may have different experiences, and discussing these issues can help them understand and feel equal. Even if you have not experienced racism directly, your children are still at risk because of their skin color or cultural background.

Racism can manifest in various forms, and one common expression is bullying in multicultural children. Studies have shown that racial bullying is a significant problem in schools and communities with diverse populations. A report by the National Center for Education Statistics in America found that over 25% of students had been bullied because of their race or ethnicity within the school system. This data highlights the distressing reality that a considerable number of multicultural children face racism-based bullying.

Addressing racism is not about instilling fear or animosity, but about empowering children to comprehend the complexities of society with empathy and knowledge. When addressing racism, it is vital to rely on accurate information and historical context. This will help your children identify racism when they are faced with it as well as know how to respond to it.

Groundwork #5: Clarify Your Family Values

Navigating diverse cultural traditions also involves understanding and clarifying your family's values. Clarifying your family values is crucial to ensure a cohesive and supportive environment for children navigating their multifaceted identities. Define your family's values to make sure your children's identities are connected to them. This not only reinforces their sense of belonging but also helps them appreciate the richness of their multicultural background. Reflect on what aspects of your cultural heritage are essential to preserve and pass down to the next generation. Incorporate cultural practices into daily routines, celebrations, and storytelling, ensuring these traditions become a natural and cherished part of your family life. By doing so, you create a strong foundation for your children to embrace their unique identities with pride and confidence.

Start by reflecting on the core principles and beliefs that are most important to you and your partner. Consider the values that have shaped your lives individually and those you wish to instill in your children. This process involves open discussions between parents about cultural traditions, religious beliefs, and moral principles from both sides of the family. By identifying and agreeing on these fundamental values, you create a unified foundation for your family, which can provide stability and guidance for your children.

Next, prioritize and integrate these values into your daily life. Mixed-race families often have the unique opportunity to blend traditions and customs from multiple cultures, creating a rich and diverse environment. This integration can be seen in various aspects of everyday life, such as the foods you cook, the holidays you celebrate, and the stories you tell. It is important to make deliberate choices about the traditions and practices to uphold, ensuring they align with your family values. For example, if respect and kindness are core values, find ways to incorporate these into your interactions and cultural practices. This deliberate integration helps your children understand and appreciate the importance of their heritage while connecting it to the core principles of your family.

Takeaways

- **Groundwork #1: Celebrating multiculturalism** helps children appreciate their unique identity and counters the negative effects of the color blindness theory, thereby fostering an environment where diversity is valued and respected.
- **Groundwork #2: Embrace Uniqueness.** Multiracial children benefit greatly from embracing their unique identities, which helps them avoid issues like low self-esteem and racial misidentification.

- **Groundwork #3: Eliminate The Stereotypes.** Children recognize racial differences from a very young age, making early conversations about race and stereotypes crucial.
- **Groundwork #4: Understand Racism.** Engaging children in discussions about racism and its impacts fosters empathy and understanding. Addressing racism early and accurately helps children recognize and respond to it proactively, empowering them to navigate and challenge discriminatory behaviors.
- **Groundwork #5: Clarify Your Family Values.** Clarifying and preserving your family's cultural values helps connect your children to their heritage.

CHAPTER 2

How to Foster Cultural Diversity

"If culture was a house, then language was the key to the front door, to all the rooms inside." — Khaled Hosseini

Cultural traditions are the vibrant threads that connect individuals to their roots and heritage. They provide a sense of belonging and identity, fostering a deeper understanding of one's place in the world. However, for multiracial children, navigating these different cultural traditions can sometimes be akin to walking on a tightrope. The fusion of diverse cultural backgrounds can lead to moments of confusion, self-doubt, and a sense of being torn between multiple identities.

As parents, we are responsible for creating an environment that celebrates the amalgamation of cultures within our families. Studies and literature on the topic have shown that the importance of guiding our children through multiracial identity struggles and the exploration of their cultural heritage must not be overlooked. We must strive to foster cultural pride, understanding and multiracial resilience in our children. Here are ways you can achieve this:

Speak Your Language: Nurturing Bilingualism in Multicultural Families

Being able to master multiple languages has numerous and obvious cognitive, social, and cultural benefits. For multicultural families, bilingualism becomes a bridge that connects them to their roots and heritage, preserving their cultural identity across generations[1]

- Language and culture are intrinsically linked; they share a symbiotic relationship.
- Language serves as a vessel for passing down customs, traditions, and values.
- Language also connects the child specifically to the native speakers and culture of that language. When parents speak their native language to their children, they transmit not only linguistic skills but also cultural knowledge, stories, and folklore.
- Through language, children gain insight into their family's history, values, and way of life.[2] Bilingual children tend to develop a broader perspective on the world and can often better appreciate different cultural nuances. They can easily engage with relatives, grandparents, and extended family members who may not speak English fluently.
- By speaking their language, parents and family members strengthen their bond with the children and create a secure foundation for cultural preservation and a feeling of belonging.

Actions you can take

1. **Continue to speak your native language** with your children. Find a study support group for kids to learn multiple languages simultaneously at a young age. When each parent speaks their language to the child, the child learns the language early on, without knowing these are two different languages.
2. **Seek supporting networks.** Schools and communities can also play a vital role in supporting bilingualism in multicultural families.
    - Many educational institutions offer language programs that cater to students' diverse linguistic backgrounds.

> Enrolling your children in these institutions will also help their journey.
> - Diverse communities also organize cultural events, language exchange programs, and storytelling sessions to learn about and preserve various languages and traditions. By searching and joining such initiatives, you can create a sense of belonging and acceptance for multicultural families, reinforcing the value of your languages and cultures.

Talk About Your History

Talking about your history and embracing the cultural traditions within a multiracial family is not only a journey of self-discovery and understanding, but also a powerful tool that can enrich your life and the lives of your children.

Exploring your family's past and cultural heritage provides you with invaluable knowledge of the various customs and values that have shaped who you are today. Understanding the roots of your heritage allows you to appreciate the rich tapestry of your family's history. It also fosters a sense of belonging as you connect with the unique experiences and stories passed down through generations.

Exploring your history is more than just learning facts and dates; it's about strengthening the bond with your family and your ancestors. When you engage in conversations with parents, grandparents, and other relatives about their experiences, you create a shared sense of belonging and unity. These intergenerational conversations can very well become cherished memories and an opportunity to pass down cultural knowledge to the younger members of the family.[3]

Actions you can take

1. **Encourage discussion on histories,** not only from your own background but all historical backgrounds. This will open their eyes to the diverse perspectives and realities of the world. As they learn about different stories, they develop empathy and compassion for people from various backgrounds.
2. **Explore family histories of both sides**, including family trees, towns they lived in, their occupations, their relationships and even dietary habits, health beliefs or medical history. This helps your children to learn not only that there are differences between the two sides of the family, but also that there are commonalities between the two. This would help strengthen family bonds, heritage pride and admiration for diversity that complements your life.

Emphasizing Both Cultures: Nurturing Cultural Balance in Multiracial Families

Just like when you talk about histories from both sides of the family, teaching children about both cultural backgrounds helps them feel pride, admiration, and knowledge of their heritage. This approach mitigates the risk of suppressing or rejecting one culture over the other. We'll explore the importance of teaching kids about both parents' cultures, the risks of neglecting the culture that may be the minority in the community, and how open conversations about these topics can benefit your multiracial children.

From the very beginning, I made a conscious effort to share the customs, traditions, and values of both sides of our family with my child. My child has been exposed to the music, food, and language of both cultures. We celebrate holidays and festivals from both backgrounds, ensuring that they experience the beauty of their dual heritage. For example, during Christmas, we incorporate traditions from both sides, decorating the tree with ornaments representing his western cultural background and celebrating Thai New Year with water, giving respect to his Buddhist heritage.

Through this exposure, I have witnessed my child develop a well-rounded understanding of his heritage. He asks questions about the significance of certain customs and shows genuine interest in learning about both cultures.

Celebrating both cultures equally reinforces the value of each heritage within the family dynamic. Parents can designate specific days to celebrate festivals and traditions from both sides. This not only enriches the family's cultural experiences but also strengthens the bond between parents and children.

For example, during the Lunar New Year, the family can engage in Chinese traditions, while on another occasion, they may celebrate Diwali or Hanukkah. By embracing these cultural festivities together, children learn to cherish and respect both their backgrounds and those of their parents.

By combining elements of both cultures into daily life, such as festivals, holidays, multiple languages, and traditional dishes, we create a multicultural environment where children can learn, experience, and embrace their heritage.

Actions you can take

1. **Introduce your children to the richness of both cultures from an early age.** Teaching them about the customs, traditions, languages, and values of both parents allows them to develop a well-rounded understanding of their heritage. This exposure

nurtures a deep appreciation for the diversity within their family, fostering a sense of cultural pride and identity.[4]

2. **Keep in mind not to neglect one of the Cultures.** Depending on which is dominant where you live, there is a risk of unintentionally neglecting the other parent's culture. The allure of the unfamiliar can lead parents to focus predominantly on one cultural background, leaving the other underrepresented. Neglecting one culture can have detrimental effects on a child's sense of identity. It may lead to feelings of disconnection, confusion, or even rejection of one part of their heritage. This can impact their self-esteem and create internal conflicts as they try to navigate their identity within the family and the broader society.[5]

3. **Create Mutual Respect.** For a peaceful cultural blend, parents must admire each other and openly communicate about their various cultures. Both parents can actively participate in sharing their cultural practices, stories, and experiences with their children. By respecting both sides of the parents' cultural heritage, children can learn to appreciate the unique aspects of both backgrounds.

4. **Encourage Open Discussions.** As you navigate this journey, engage in open and honest conversations about your cultural backgrounds with your children. Expect their questions and address any curiosity they may have about their heritage. Encourage them to ask questions and explore their cultural identities freely. By fostering an environment of open communication, you create a safe space for your children to embrace their uniqueness.

Have Multicultural Experiences

Having a household that celebrates multicultural experiences is a thrilling and rewarding way to broaden your child's understanding of diversity. Participating in various cultural activities as a family not only offers enjoyable moments of togetherness but also helps to expand your family's outlook and dispel preconceptions.

Engaging in new cultural experiences benefits not only your child but the entire family. As you explore diverse traditions and engage with people from various backgrounds, you embark on a journey of discovery together. Each encounter provides an opportunity to learn more about yourself, others, and the world around you.[6]

Actions you can take

1. **Participate in cultural events and activities as a family.** This can be an enjoyable and insightful way to learn about different traditions and customs. Attend local festivals, cultural exhibitions, or food fairs that celebrate the heritage of various communities. As you immerse yourselves in these events, your child will witness the beauty of diversity firsthand.[7]
2. **Expose your child to a range of multicultural experiences.** This can be through traditional holidays, a variety of food, music, dance or art exhibitions. This can help challenge and break down stereotypes. When your child interacts with individuals from different backgrounds and engages in their cultural practices, it humanizes those cultures and dispels misconceptions. This firsthand encounter fosters a deeper understanding of the complexity and richness of each culture.[8]
3. **Encourage your child to ask questions and engage in conversations with locals.** This direct interaction not only builds social skills but also deepens their understanding and appreciation for the community's history and values.

Provide Tools To Connect With People

According to a study conducted by Michigan State University, children expand their thinking by making connections.[9] Exposing them to games, books, shows, and movies that feature people who look like them can help boost their pride in their background.

> ### Actions you can take
>
> 1. Make sure your child has **access to media that reflects their heritage**. It shows them that people who share their heritage are out there doing all sorts of positive things and going through similar experiences. It also teaches them that they have things in common with people who may not look like them.
> 2. You can also **incorporate cultural elements into playdates** with your child and their friends. Encourage them to share their expertise in cultural crafts, games or foods, or take their friends to culturally significant locations nearby. It's a great way for your child to showcase their culture and create meaningful connections with their friends.[10]

Discuss Images in the Media

We live in a time when the media is more diverse than ever, showcasing various cultural backgrounds, ethnicities, and experiences. This inclusivity is a positive step towards fostering understanding and empathy among different communities. Children are exposed to characters and stories that differ from their own, opening doors to learning about various cultures. However, it's important to note that amid this diversity, some portrayals can perpetuate negative stereotypes, which can have a lasting impact.

Think about it – have you ever noticed that certain characters or groups of people are often depicted in a less appealing light than others? These unfavorable stereotypes can reinforce biases and misconceptions, even in young minds. As parents, caregivers, and mentors, we need to be aware of the media content our children are exposed to. This isn't about censorship, but rather about actively engaging with what our children see and helping them understand the nuances.

Actions you can take

1. Engaging your elementary-aged child in **discussions about media representations** can be a valuable learning experience. Encourage them to question why certain portrayals may be unjust or incorrect. Ask them to critically analyze the messages conveyed through images. By fostering these conversations, you empower your child to think critically about what they see and challenge harmful stereotypes.
2. Help your children **connect the dots between media, stereotypes, and real-life interactions.** Watch and Discuss Together. **Media Analysis**: Watch a show together and then discuss the characters and their cultural representations. Ask questions like, "Do you know anyone like this character? How are they similar or different?"
3. **Approach the media with a critical and open mind**. Engaging with your children about media portrayals can spark meaningful conversations about culture, representation, and empathy. By guiding them to think critically about what they see and teaching them to recognize harmful stereotypes, you're helping them become conscious consumers of the media.

Explore Books and other Resources

Books are another powerful tool that can spark meaningful conversations about diversity. By strategically using books as a tool to explore diversity, you can help your child develop a lifelong appreciation for the richness that different cultures, languages, and viewpoints offer to the world.

Other resources include movies, documentaries, TV shows, games and other media sources.

Actions you can take

1. **Seek out literature that explores various cultures, languages, and viewpoints.** Include a variety of formats in your reading list—picture books, novels, biographies, and folklore from around the world. It can be in book format, movie format or cartoon format. This variety can cater to different age levels and reading abilities, and it provides a broader spectrum of viewpoints and storytelling styles. Each format offers unique benefits and learning opportunities, from the visual storytelling of picture books to the in-depth exploration found in novels and biographies.
2. **Involve your child in the process of choosing these books and other resources.** This can be an engaging way to explore their interests and questions about different cultures and identities.
3. **When selecting what to read or watch, consider both the story and the storyteller.** Opt for books written by authors from diverse backgrounds to ensure authenticity in representation. This encourages your child to hear voices and experiences from the actual perspectives of those who live them. Choose stories that celebrate diversity, challenge stereotypes, and introduce new perspectives.

4. **Reading together not only enhances your child's reading skills but also fosters empathy and understanding.** Encourage them to ask questions and express their thoughts on the stories and characters they encounter. This active engagement helps to solidify the lessons learned from the books and makes the experience more memorable.

5. **Don't shy away from books or other resources that discuss the challenges related to race and diversity.** Children are remarkably perceptive and can handle complex topics. Books that address these issues thoughtfully can prompt important discussions about fairness, justice, and how to support others who face discrimination.

6. **Complement your reading or watching sessions with activities that reinforce the messages in the books or movies.** This might include arts and crafts inspired by the stories, cooking recipes from the cultures depicted, or even attending local cultural events. These activities help bring the stories to life and give your child tangible experiences of diverse cultures.

List of Recommended Books and Other Resources

Picture Books for Younger Children

1. *The Colors of Us* by Karen Katz
   A wonderful story that celebrates the different skin tones of children around the world. It's a great way to introduce young kids to the beauty of diversity.

2. *Marisol McDonald Doesn't Match / Marisol McDonald no Combina* by Monica Brown

This bilingual book tells the story of a young girl who embraces her unique mixed-race heritage and shows that it's okay to be different.

3. ***Same, Same but Different*** by Jenny Sue Kostecki-Shaw
A lovely picture book about two boys from different countries who discover that while their worlds are very different, they also have many similarities.

4. ***Mixed: A Colorful Story*** by Arree Chung
This vibrant book uses colors to tell a story about diversity, acceptance, and unity, making it perfect for young readers.

Middle-Grade Books

5. ***Blended*** by Sharon M. Draper
A poignant story about a biracial girl who navigates the complexities of having parents of different races and cultures.

6. ***Stella Díaz Has Something to Say*** by Angela Dominguez
This book follows a young girl of Mexican American heritage as she learns to navigate her identity and find her voice.

7. ***Inside Out and Back Again*** by Thanhhà Lai
Though not explicitly about a mixed-race child, this book beautifully captures the experience of cultural identity through the eyes of a young Vietnamese girl immigrating to America.

8. ***October Sky*** by Homer Hickam
This memoir tells the story of Homer Hickam, a boy from a coal mining town in West Virginia who dreams of launching rockets. Inspired by the launch of Sputnik in 1957, Hickam and his friends form a rocket club and pursue their passion for rocketry against

the odds. With determination and the support of their community and a dedicated teacher, they achieve remarkable success.

9. ***It Ain't So Awful, Falafel*** by Firoozeh Dumas
    Set in the late 1970s, this humorous and poignant story follows Zomorod (Cindy) Yousefzadeh, an Iranian American middle schooler trying to fit in and make friends while dealing with the Iranian Revolution and its impact on her family.

10. ***Half and Half*** by Lensey Namioka
    Fiona Cheng, who is half Chinese and half Scottish, feels torn between her two cultures. Her struggle becomes even more complicated when her two grandmothers come to visit and try to pull her in different directions.

11. ***Brown Girl Dreaming*** by Jacqueline Woodson
    This memoir recounts Woodson's experiences growing up as an African American in the 1960s and 1970s, dealing with the complexities of her family's heritage and the broader social changes of the time.

12. ***Genesis Begins Again*** by Alicia D. Williams
    Thirteen-year-old Genesis Anderson is constantly being reminded of her dark skin and her family's financial struggles. As she tries to lighten her skin, she learns to embrace her true self and her heritage.

Young Adult Books

13. ***The Absolutely True Diary of a Part-Time Indian*** by Sherman Alexie
    This novel explores the life of a Native American teenager who transfers to an all-white school, delving into themes of identity and belonging.

14. *Hidden Figures* by Margot Lee Shetterly
    This inspiring book tells the true story of four African American women mathematicians at NASA who played crucial roles in some of the greatest achievements in space exploration. It highlights their groundbreaking work and the challenges they overcame in a racially and gender-biased society.

15. *American Born Chinese* by Gene Luen Yang
    A graphic novel that intertwines three stories, exploring Chinese American identity and the challenges of fitting in.

16. *Everything, Everything* by Nicola Yoon
    This novel tells the story of a biracial girl who is allergic to everything, exploring themes of identity, love, and breaking free from constraints.

17. *The Hate U Give* by Angie Thomas
    Though it deals with broader themes of race and identity in America, the protagonist's mixed-race background adds depth to the story's exploration of belonging and justice.

Non-Fiction and Biographies

18. *Dreams from My Father: A Story of Race and Inheritance* by Barack Obama
    While more suitable for older teens and adults, this memoir explores President Obama's biracial identity and his journey of self-discovery.

19. *Amina's Voice* by Hena Khan
    This book captures the struggles of a Pakistani American girl as she navigates her cultural identity and friendships.
    These books can help mixed-race kids see themselves reflected in literature and understand that their diverse backgrounds are

something to be celebrated. They also provide great opportunities for discussions about identity, culture, and acceptance.

Books for Parents

1. ***Does Anybody Else Look Like Me? A Parent's Guide to Raising Multiracial Children*** by Donna Jackson Nakazawa
   A guide for parents on how to support their mixed-race children's identity development.

2. ***Parenting in the Eye of the Storm: The Adoptive Parent's Guide to Navigating the Teen Years*** by Katie Naftzger
   Useful for adoptive parents of mixed-race children, providing strategies for dealing with identity and belonging issues during the teen years.

Websites and Organizations

1. **Project RACE (Reclassify All Children Equally)**: An advocacy group dedicated to securing multiracial classifications on all school forms and documents.

2. **MAVIN Foundation**: Focuses on the mixed-race experience and provides resources for families and educators.

3. **Multiracial Americans of Southern California (MASC)**: Offers support and resources for multiracial individuals and families.

Tv Shows

1. ***Mixed-ish*** (2019-2021)
   A prequel spin-off of "Black-ish," this show follows Rainbow Johnson's experiences growing up in a mixed-race family during

the 1980s. The show is from the American ABC network, created by Kenya Barris, Tracee Ellis Ross and Peter Saji.

2. ***Black-ish*** (2014-2022)
   While not solely focused on mixed-race issues, this show frequently explores themes of race, identity, and culture through the lens of an African American family, including Rainbow Johnson's mixed-race background.

3. ***Dear White People*** (2017-2021)
   This series delves into the racial tensions and identity struggles of a diverse group of college students, including several mixed-race characters.

4. ***The Fosters*** (2013-2018)
   A family drama featuring a diverse and blended family, including mixed-race children, dealing with a range of social issues.

5. ***Atypical*** (2017-2021)
   While the show primarily focuses on autism, it includes a subplot involving a mixed-race relationship and explores related identity issues.

Movies

1. ***1000% Me, Growing Up Mixed*** (2023) Documentary
   W. Kamau Bell directs this easygoing, funny and original HBO-documentary about race, mixed race, position and identity in the San Francisco Bay area.

2. ***Loving*** (2016)
   Based on the true story of Richard and Mildred Loving, an interracial couple whose marriage led to a landmark Supreme Court decision invalidating laws prohibiting interracial marriage.

3. ***Everything, Everything*** (2017)
   A romantic drama about a young woman with a rare disease who falls in love with her new neighbor, exploring themes of love and identity in a mixed-race context.

4. ***The Sun Is Also a Star*** (2019)
   A romance between a Jamaican girl and a Korean American boy, exploring themes of immigration, identity, and cultural heritage.

5. ***To All the Boys I've Loved Before*** (2018-2021)
   Follows Lara Jean Covey, a Korean American teenager navigating high school and relationships, highlighting aspects of her mixed-race identity.

6. ***Blended*** (2014)
   A comedy featuring a blended family dynamic with mixed-race children, exploring the challenges and joys of family integration.

7. ***The Half of It*** (2020)
   A coming-of-age story about a shy, introverted Chinese American student who helps a jock write love letters to a girl they both secretly love, delving into themes of cultural identity and self-discovery.

CHAPTER 3

How to Help Your Children Build Confidence

"If you judge people, you have no time to love them." — Mother Teresa

Observing the intricate patterns of friendship among children of different races during the mid-childhood years can be both gratifying and difficult. As parents, you must be alert to recognize the signs that something might be amiss in your child's interactions with friends. Pay attention to changes in behavior or attitude, as they could indicate challenges in their friendships.

Every child is unique, so what works for one may not work for another. The key is to foster an open line of communication with your child, where they feel comfortable sharing their experiences. If parents do not start discussions with their children about these topics, children may be left to manage complicated friendship issues without guidance and to the great detriment of these relationships.

Building Inner Confidence

Social interactions play a pivotal role in shaping a child's sense of self during early childhood. Parents of multiracial children must pay close attention to how their kids navigate these social interactions. We need to pay attention to the balance of fostering inner confidence in grade schoolers, addressing the challenges they may face in making friends, and the importance of creating an open and welcoming environment. Parents are recommended to be attuned to their child's social experiences. Children who struggle to make friends and fail to develop close, trusting relationships are at a higher risk of experiencing low self-esteem and even depression.[1]

We need to actively participate in our children's journey of building inner confidence. By fostering competencies, nurturing passions, and embracing the learning process, you contribute to the development of resilient and self-assured individuals ready to face the challenges that come their way.

Actions you can take

1. As parents, our role extends beyond providing material support; **we must also be emotional anchors**, helping our children navigate the often-turbulent waters of peer relationships. To build inner confidence, we need to emphasize awareness and allow space for our children to develop relationships independently. We want to be tuned into their social experiences without micromanaging their interactions. This involves being observant without being intrusive and offering guidance without imposing control. We will talk more about how we can guide them to navigate through the different challenges later in this chapter.
2. Anecdotal evidence suggests that **opening up our homes and welcoming our children's friends for playdates can be a powerful way to foster social connections**. Creating an environment where friends feel comfortable and accepted encourages positive social interactions. Share stories with your child about your own experiences with friendship, emphasizing the value of diversity in these relationships.
3. Your child expressing hesitation or reluctance about inviting a friend over could be an opportunity for a candid conversation. Ask open-ended questions, allowing your child to express

their feelings and concerns. This interactive approach fosters a sense of trust and openness, reinforcing that their emotions are valid and valued.

4. One fundamental aspect of cultivating inner confidence is encouraging and supporting our children's interests and passions. Whether it's art, sports, music, or any other pursuit, finding what resonates with our children and actively supporting their endeavors contributes significantly to their overall confidence. Research indicates that when children are engaged in activities they are passionate about, it positively impacts their self-esteem.[2]

5. By actively encouraging and facilitating their participation, you not only provide an avenue for skill development but also foster a sense of accomplishment. As parents, we become their cheerleaders, celebrating their achievements and reinforcing the idea that they are capable and valued.

Navigating Friendships

One common issue that comes up is when friends say hurtful things, particularly related to race and identity. Imagine your child coming home upset after a friend made a comment that left them feeling hurt and confused. In these moments, children need guidance on how to handle such situations. And having the right words can make all the difference.

As you engage in these conversations, try to keep your tone interactive, anecdotal, and supportive. Encourage your child to ask questions and share their thoughts, creating a safe space for them to express themselves. By doing so, you not only address the immediate issue of hurtful comments but also lay the foundation for ongoing discussions about identity and diversity.

The goal here is not just to settle issues as they arise but also to give your child the assurance that they can handle relationships and remain true to themselves in the years to come. This area focuses on developing a strong foundation of resilience, self-awareness, and self-confidence to help your child handle any obstacles they may experience on their journey of discovering their identity in a diverse environment.

Actions you can take

1. It's essential to equip your child with the language to effectively communicate. By providing them with different ways to describe themselves, you empower them to express their identity confidently. Encourage your child to articulate their feelings and experiences, letting them know they have the right to define themselves on their terms.

2. Offer your child a range of self-prescribed labels, allowing them to choose how they want to be identified. Encourage combining aspects of their identity into a new label that feels right for them. Let them create a hybrid label that uniquely represents their identity. Example: "You're part Japanese and part Hispanic. You can call yourself Jap-Spanic or something else that feels right to you," or "You've lived in both New York and Tokyo. Maybe you'd like to identify as a New York-Tokyo kid or something else that reflects both places." This not only empowers them but also prepares them for instances where others may struggle to comprehend their unique identity. Monoracial children, in particular, might find it challenging to understand the multiracial complexities that come with self-identification. By arming your child with the ability to express their identity, you give them the tools to stand up for themselves confidently.

3. Share stories about your own experiences, emphasizing the importance of embracing diversity and being proud of who

> they are. Make it clear that being different is a strength, not a weakness.

Navigating "Subtle Acts of Exclusion" (SAE)

The concept of SAE is described by Tiffany Jana and Michael Baran in the book *"Subtle Acts of Exclusion: How to Understand, Identify, and Stop Microaggressions."* It describes how subtle acts by very well-meaning people can sometimes be perceived negatively by the recipient, however well-intended the comment or act might be.[3]

One of the examples given, in an American context, is about a Korean American woman who felt uncomfortable and annoyed when her Caucasian coworker, while trying to be friendly during lunch, mistakenly assumed she could comment on Thai food. When she clarified that she wasn't from Thailand, he continued to inquire about her background. She said she was from Chicago but had to explain her Korean heritage due to her Asian features. The coworker's response, "Oh, so close," highlighted his misunderstanding and the assumption that Asian cultures are similar. This interaction underscores the frequent and tiresome need for people of Asian descent to explain their heritage in the American context.

Another example is two coworkers, one black and one white, who became close friends and often had lunch together. During a conversation, the black coworker mentioned her perspective as a black person, to which the white coworker responded, "Oh, but I don't even think of you as black." This upset the black coworker, who expressed that she wanted to be recognized as black to feel connected to her demographic. The white coworker tried to clarify, saying he saw her as an individual rather than her race. However, the black coworker felt invisible and believed that ignoring her racial identity indicated a racial bias

While these examples are not specifically about mixed-race people, they are relevant as these same situations often happen to mixed-race individuals.

Actions you can take

1. What's important to understand about these interactions is the intent. Let your children know that, normally, people do not engage in these situations with bad intentions. Most of the time, they just want to be friendly and connect. Other times, it is because they are curious. They want to get to know the person they are talking to, and the general unfamiliarity makes them think they are engaging in a friendly and positive way.

2. Teach your children that they could choose to clarify and explain how the question made them feel. They could say something like: "Hold on a minute, I get asked that question a lot. This question makes me feel a certain way." Do not let it slide as that may likely occur again. Instead, they can calmly explain and help the other person understand, but remember to be respectful, noting that the other person is well-meaning. Do not approach this from a blame-passing viewpoint or scold the person for trying to engage and make a connection. The goal here is to create mutual understanding and to acknowledge the intent of the comment. The goal is not to make the speaker uncomfortable or feel bad about their comment but rather to educate them so they are conscious of the impact of their words on your children. This will help your children to connect with others on a deeper level and foster better understanding.

3. Research has shown that providing children with scripts and phrases empowers them to respond assertively to such challenging situations.[4] But do not just tell your child what to say during situations like this. Rather, involve them in creating their response. This will help to increase their confidence

> and make them authentic in their interactions. You are also empowering them to take ownership of their narrative, reinforcing the idea that their self-perception is valid and important.
>
> 4. It's important to emphasize to our children that the goal is not necessarily to convince others but to deflect and stop hurtful interactions. This distinction is crucial for their emotional well-being, as it shifts the focus from seeking external validation to prioritizing their sense of self-worth.

Navigating around Racial Bias

Children absorb information from their surroundings, with parents and caregivers being their first and most influential teachers in understanding racial disparities. For example, in Adam's school, a safe space for discussing cultural discrimination was created, promoting inclusivity and empathy. This empowered students to address prejudice actively. Teaching cultural diversity and encouraging dialogues about bias help combat discrimination by celebrating diversity. Media and social environments also significantly shape their understanding, often reinforcing stereotypes. Schools play a vital role, and educators are essential in promoting inclusivity. As children grow, their understanding of racial bias evolves, and proactive guidance from parents can help them become thoughtful and compassionate. Parents must be aware of their own biases, model inclusive behavior, and address any biases to shape children's attitudes positively.

Confronting our own racial bias is an ongoing process that requires self-reflection and a willingness to challenge our assumptions. It is normal to have biases, as they are shaped by societal influences and personal experiences. However, it is essential to continuously educate ourselves and question these biases to create a more inclusive environment for our children.

Actions you can take

1. To help your child process racial bias, you must first address and confront your own biases, including stereotyping, intersectionality, and status discrimination. After doing so, you can effectively promote inclusivity and teach your children to embrace diversity.
2. Be a role model for your children by treating everyone with respect and fairness, regardless of their cultural background. Since children learn by observing their parents and caregivers, be mindful of your attitudes and language when discussing people from different ethnicities or races.[5]
3. Surround yourself with a diverse group of friends and acquaintances from various cultural backgrounds to broaden your perspective and challenge preconceived notions or stereotypes.
4. Take your kids on trips to explore different cultures by visiting museums, cultural events, and local communities, allowing them to experience the richness of various traditions and practices firsthand.
5. Get involved in your child's school, place of worship, and politics by participating in multicultural events, workshops, and discussions. This interaction helps you gain insights into diverse cultures and perspectives.

How to Help Your Children Through Identity Crisis: The Infamous "What Are You?" Question

"Our job as parents is to help our children understand that their rich, multifaceted identities are something to be proud of, not something to hide or feel ashamed about." — Donna Jackson Nakazawa[1]

Navigating the complexities of teenage life, the multiracial teen often finds themselves grappling with a daunting question: "Where do I truly belong?"

The adolescent years are inherently riddled with identity crises, but for multiracial children, the struggle is deeper. As friendships evolve and social circles tighten, the pressure to align with a specific racial identity becomes an unwavering force. Unlike their monoracial peers, these multiracial teenagers find themselves caught in a web of perplexity, attempting to reconcile the various sides of their heritage.

Donna J. Nakasawa's *"The Five Steps of Multiracial Identity Formation"* explores the complex journey of forming a multiracial identity. The process begins with the child's desire to establish their own identity separate from their racial heritage. However, as societal pressures increase, the challenge of categorizing oneself into a specific racial group becomes daunting. Influenced by peers and societal expectations, adolescents may struggle to find a sense of belonging due to their unique racial background. Some may overemphasize one aspect of their heritage in an attempt to fit in, which can lead to exclusion or bullying of those from different ethnic backgrounds. This struggle can widen the gap between the conflicting components of their identity.

This section explores the troubles teenagers of multiple races face and illuminates the poignant trek of coming to terms with yourself amid social assumptions and the influence of friends.

Nurturing Identity: A Sympathetic Guide for Parents

This guide highlights the crucial role parents play in helping their multiracial teens develop a positive and complex racial identity. Here are practical steps and strategies for parents:

1. **Foster Positive Self-Esteem**
   - Encourage teens to embrace their multiracial heritage.
   - Highlight the strengths and uniqueness of having multiple racial backgrounds.
2. **Acknowledge and Embrace Multiple Racial Identities**
   - Recognize the importance of embracing all aspects of their racial identity.
   - Understand that this can positively impact their mental health.
3. **Encourage Open Communication**
   - Talk openly about the complex emotions related to their identity.
   - Affirm their feelings and experiences to build confidence.
4. **Support Appreciation of Racial Roots**
   - Help teens appreciate and value their heritage from both sides of their family.
   - Use educational activities and family discussions to deepen their understanding.
5. **Facilitate Integration of Racial Heritages**
   - Guide them in blending their racial backgrounds into a unified, authentic self-concept.

- Provide consistent support throughout this integration process.
6. **Practice Active Listening and Grant Autonomy**
   - Listen actively without immediately trying to solve every problem.
   - Allow teens to have autonomy in exploring and defining their identity.
7. **Research-Backed Insights**
   - Utilize research and studies to inform your approach to supporting your child.
   - Understand the various stages of identity formation and provide appropriate support at each stage.

By following these steps, parents can help their multiracial teens navigate their identity development with confidence and authenticity.

Multiracial Identity and Its Challenges

Understanding and supporting multiracial identity involves recognizing the unique challenges multiracial teens face. Here are practical ways to help:

1. **Acknowledge the Problem**
   - Recognize and validate your child's experiences and struggles. This lets them know their feelings are real and important.
2. **Open Dialogue**
   - Discuss the difficulties openly. This builds trust and encourages teens to share their feelings.
3. **Handling Official Forms**
   - Prepare your child for situations where they must select a single race on forms. Discuss the option of choosing "other" and emphasize the value of their diverse heritage.

4. **Dealing with the "What Are You?" Question**
   - Help your child develop confident responses to questions about their identity.
   - Avoid fractional descriptions (e.g., "half black and half indigenous") to prevent feelings of division.
5. **Embrace Fluid Identity**
   - Accept that your child may identify differently in various social contexts. This adaptability is a positive trait.
6. **Model Positive Behavior**
   - Share your own background and experiences to show the value of diversity.
   - Treat everyone with respect and teach your child to do the same.
7. **Encourage Learning and Curiosity**
   - Create an environment where your child feels comfortable asking about different cultures and backgrounds.
   - Celebrate various cultural traditions and participate in multicultural events.
8. **Challenge Stereotypes**
   - Address and discuss stereotypes and biases when they arise. Use these moments as educational opportunities.
9. **Show Empathy and Discuss Diversity**
   - Talk about news and events related to diversity with empathy. Help your child understand different perspectives and emotions.
10. **Promote Diverse Friendships**
    - Encourage friendships with peers from diverse backgrounds.

Research Insights

- **Dr. Maria P. P. Root** emphasizes the importance of acknowledging the challenges multiracial people face to foster open dialogue and trust.

- **American Psychological Association (APA)** research highlights the impact of racial categorization on psychological well-being and the need for proactive support.
- **The National Association of School Psychologists (NASP)** suggests that awareness and education about multiracial identity contribute to inclusive and empathetic environments.
- **Dr. Kelly F. Jackson's** research shows that having an adaptable racial identity is normal and beneficial in varying social circumstances.

Practical Advice

- **Start Conversations Early**: Begin discussions about race and identity at a young age to build a strong foundation.
- **Promote Self-Exploration**: Allow your child the autonomy to explore and define their identity.
- **Be a Supportive Listener**: Listen actively to your child's experiences without trying to solve every problem immediately.

By following these steps, you can help your multiracial teen navigate their identity development with confidence and authenticity.

How to Support The Chosen Minority Identity

Modeling positive behavior is a powerful way to teach children about the importance of embracing diversity. As parents, caregivers, and role models, your actions speak louder than words. Here are some ways to demonstrate positive responses to diversity:

- *Embrace Your Own Uniqueness*: Emphasize that everyone has qualities that make them special. Share your own stories of how your background and experiences have shaped you. This encourages children to appreciate their own identities and value diversity in others.

- *Be Respectful*: Treat everyone with respect, regardless of their differences. Teach your child the golden rule – *treat others the way you want to be treated*. Show them that kindness knows no boundaries.
- *Encourage Questions*: Children are naturally curious. Encourage them to ask questions about others' cultures, experiences, and backgrounds. Provide accurate and age-appropriate information, fostering an environment of learning and understanding.[2]
- *Celebrate Differences*: Highlight the beauty of diversity by celebrating various cultural holidays, traditions, and observances. Participating in multicultural events and activities can broaden your child's horizons.
- *Challenge Stereotypes*: Address stereotypes and biases when they arise. Use these moments as opportunities to discuss why stereotypes are harmful and how they perpetuate unfair judgments.[3]
- *Show Empathy*: When discussing news or events related to diversity and inclusion, demonstrate empathy for those affected. Help your child understand the emotions of others and how they might feel in similar situations.
- *Encourage Friendship*: Encourage your child to make friends with peers from diverse backgrounds. Genuine friendships can dismantle biases and cultivate a deep appreciation for different cultures.[4]

By employing these practices, you, as parents, create a tangible model of positive responses to diversity. Children absorb these lessons not just through words, but by observing how their parents interact with the world.

CHAPTER 5

How to Overcome Challenges for Parents & Their Multiracial Relationship

"Love recognizes no barriers. It jumps hurdles, leaps fences, penetrates walls to arrive at its destination full of hope." — Maya Angelou

Relationships of any kind can be both exciting and intimidating but cross-cultural relationships are particularly unique. They offer a rich collection of experiences and learning opportunities for all parties involved but can also present their own challenges. As parents, you need to provide your multiracial kids with the resources and understanding they need to confront any issues that may come up in cross-cultural relationships. This involves teaching them the importance of empathy, open communication, and respect for different cultural perspectives. Encourage them to learn about and celebrate the diverse backgrounds of their friends and partners, fostering a sense of curiosity and appreciation for differences. Equip them with strategies for handling misunderstandings or conflicts that may arise due to cultural differences, emphasizing the value of patience and compromise. By providing this support, you help them build strong, respectful, and enriching relationships that honor the diverse fabric of their identities.

As parents and caregivers, our attitudes and behaviors significantly influence our children's perceptions and interactions with people from different backgrounds. And the best way to do this starts by examining yourself.

Examining Yourself

Children are remarkably perceptive, often picking up on subtle cues from their surroundings. If you display discomfort or unease when interacting with individuals from diverse backgrounds, your child is likely to mimic these behaviors. Being mindful of your reactions to others, especially to your significant other, can pave the way for open-mindedness and acceptance in your child's interactions.

Actions you can take

1. Think about how you describe or talk about your partner. Our words hold immense power. How we describe and discuss people from different cultures shapes our children's attitudes as well as your relationship with your partner. Are you using respectful and inclusive language? Are you avoiding stereotypes and generalizations? Reflect on the words you use as they influence both your child and your relationship with your partner.
2. Be truthful with yourself about your areas of improvement. We are not immune to biases, but acknowledging and addressing them is crucial. Reflect on your own biases and areas where you can improve. Admitting these weaknesses is the first step towards creating a more inclusive environment for your child.
3. Be aware of any inconsistencies between your intentions and your behaviors, and work to align them. Your words may be welcoming but is your body language welcoming? Sometimes, we say one thing and give an impression of another.

Respect for Individual Identity

No matter the cultural background, it's crucial to remind them that everyone possesses a unique individual identity different from their cultural one. Each party needs to acknowledge and value their partner as a person first—admiring interests, capabilities, and ambitions. Encourage them to support personal growth and self-expression, acknowledging the influence of culture while respecting each other's individuality. This approach fosters trust and allows the relationship to flourish.[1]

Actions you can take

1. Recognize and respect their unique hobbies, skills, and aspirations that may not necessarily align with your culture.
2. Encourage open discussions about personal dreams and goals. Celebrate the individual ambitions of each partner, supporting one another in personal endeavors regardless of cultural expectations.
3. Encourage dual appreciation—of both the cultural and the personal. This helps build a balanced relationship where both partners feel valued for who they are as well as for their cultural contributions.

Bridging the Cultural Gap

In the realm of intercultural relationships, a significant challenge lies in bridging the cultural divide between partners. It's more than just recognizing cultural differences; it's about embracing them and discovering common ground.

Actions you can take

1. Have **open communication** with your partner about various cultural practices, traditions, values, beliefs and aspirations. The goal isn't merely tolerating differences; it's celebrating them. Encourage each other to learn the other's background. This will not only help to minimize misunderstanding, but also build deeper connections in your relationships and foster mutual respect and appreciation for one another.

2. Discuss with your partner early in the relationship various topics like where each of you wants to live, how to handle finances, what traditions each wishes to uphold or create, and how each of you envisions raising any potential children. This could involve blending holiday traditions, deciding on a bilingual home environment, or supporting dual citizenship, if applicable. It's important that these decisions are made together, reflecting mutual respect and balanced incorporation of both cultural identities.

3. Practice **Active Listening** with each other. This skill is crucial in appreciating the subtleties of your partner's expressions and the unspoken elements of communication that are often culturally rooted.

4. Have plenty of **patience and empathy**. This is needed in any relationship but even more so in multiracial relationships, where there are many more opportunities for clashes due to differences in beliefs, values, etc.

5. **Learning to speak their partner's language**, even at a basic level, shows a deep level of respect and commitment to the relationship. Each can start with simple, achievable goals, such as learning basic greetings, common phrases, or expressions of affection in the partner's language. Even these small steps can significantly impact the relationship, showing respect for your partner's heritage and easing communication in more personal settings.

6. Each can gradually take on more complex language tasks as you progress, perhaps enrolling in formal language classes or using language learning apps to improve your proficiency. This deeper dive into the language will help all parties understand nuances and cultural contexts that influence their partner's thoughts and behaviors.
7. Practicing the language together can be a fun and engaging activity that strengthens relationships. It can include practical language use in everyday situations, like shopping or dining out, or through more structured activities like language games or watching films in the other's language.

Embracing Multilingual and Multicultural Experiences

Parents can encourage their child to participate in multilingual and multicultural activities, but it speaks more if the parents also take part in these activities. Participating in events that celebrate both cultures, such as festivals, language classes or cultural workshops, provides an invaluable platform for each person to explore and appreciate the other's culture. These shared experiences allow partners to immerse themselves in each other's traditions and celebrate the diversity that each brings to the relationship.

Actions you can take

1. **Attending cultural events together** not only deepens your understanding but also helps you see the beauty of your partner's traditions firsthand, fostering a deeper sense of connection.[2] This shared journey can transform appreciation into a more profound connection, as each partner witnesses the love and respect the other shows for their culture.

> 2. Encourage each other to regularly **incorporate elements from both cultures** in your daily lives. This might include cooking meals from each other's traditional cuisines, watching movies in each other's languages, or decorating the house to celebrate important cultural holidays together.

Building a Support Network of Other Cross-Cultural Couples

Another valuable strategy for enhancing cross-cultural relationships is to build a support network made up of others who are also navigating the complexities of a multiracial relationship. This network can provide a sense of community and a source of practical advice and emotional support.

Actions you can take

1. **Connect with other cross-cultural couples** through community groups, online forums, or social events.
2. Make it a safe space and share with others your experiences, solutions or tips to common challenges that arise in cross-cultural relationships. Hearing how others handle similar situations can provide both reassurance and innovative strategies that might not have been considered.
3. Organize group activities that allow you to connect with other multiracial children as well as for your children to connect with other children from cross-cultural backgrounds. This helps both you and your children gain a broader perspective and find collective wisdom that empowers all to navigate each of their unique journeys more confidently.

Conclusion

As we conclude this exploration into raising multiracial children in a diverse world, you will hopefully agree that the journey is both challenging and profoundly enriching. Multiracial children are at risk of facing several issues that do not exist for other children, and so our role as parents of multiracial children is to provide them with the right support to navigate whatever situations they may face in their everyday lives. With this book I have offered the best insights and practical advice I have found on how you can support your children through the complexities of their identities, fostering a sense of pride and belonging in a world that is rich in diversity. I have shared my personal experiences as well as the experiences of others to provide you with the best tools for raising children who are culturally self-aware and empowered to live their best life.

The strategies discussed—from encouraging open communications and leveraging books, cultural activities and other resources to encouraging empathy and understanding to navigating the nuances of cross-cultural relationships and balancing the roles of the different cultures—serve as a roadmap for parents striving to create an inclusive environment for their children. These approaches not only help multiracial children embrace their own heritages but also teach them to appreciate and respect diversity in others.

You can contribute to a more compassionate world by raising children who are comfortable with and curious about differences. The values of empathy, respect, and inclusivity are crucial as our global community becomes increasingly interconnected. By encouraging open dialogue about culture and identity and modeling respect for diversity, you are equipping your children with the tools they need to thrive in and contribute positively to this diverse world.

As you implement the ideas within these pages, remember that every small step contributes to your child's understanding and acceptance of themselves and others. You may encounter uncertainties and challenges on the way but be assured that the rewards of raising confident, culturally-aware children are immense. These children will grow up to be adults who not only navigate their own identities with confidence but also enrich the communities they become part of. They will grow up appreciating the investments you made to help them become whole humans who know their place in the community.

Your role as a parent is powerful, and you have taken a bold step by reading this book to the end. It shows your commitment to building confident multiracial children who will grow to be compassionate and self-aware individuals. Together, with each of us playing our roles, we make the world a better place, one that is safe for us and our kids.

And finally, I want to thank you for allowing me to guide you through this book's pages. I hope you have great experiences raising powerful children in today's diverse world!

References

CHAPTER 1

1. Armstrong, A. (2020). *How to Support Young Learners in Racially Diverse Classrooms*. Edutopia. Retrieved June 3, 2023, from https://www.edutopia.org/article/how-support-young-learners-racially-diverse-classrooms/
2. Hud-Aleem, R., & Countryman, J. (2008). *Biracial Identity Development and Recommendations in Therapy*. NCBI. Retrieved June 3, 2023, from https://www.ncbi.nlm.nih.gov/pmc/articles/PMC2695719/
3. Eng, J. (2021, February 11). *Why you shouldn't teach your kids to be "colorblind" - ParentsTogether*. Parents Together. Retrieved June 3, 2023, from https://parents-together.org/why-you-shouldnt-teach-your-kids-to-be-colorblind/
4. Suttie, J. (2017, March 23). *Five Ways to Reduce Racial Bias in Your Children*. Greater Good Science Center. Retrieved June 3, 2023, from https://greatergood.berkeley.edu/article/item/five_ways_to_reduce_racial_bias_in_your_children

CHAPTER 2

1. The Editors of Encyclopedia Britannica. (2009, January 30). Bilingualism | Language Acquisition, Cognitive Benefits & Education. Encyclopedia Britannica. https://www.britannica.com/topic/bilingualism
2. Tektigul, Z., Bayadilova-Altybayev, A., Sadykova, S., Iskindirova, S., Kushkimbayeva, A., & Zhumagul, D. (2023). Language is a symbol system that carries culture. International Journal of Society, Culture & Language, 11(1), 203-214.

3. Evans-Campbell, T. (2008). Historical trauma in American Indian/ Native Alaska communities: A multilevel framework for exploring impacts on individuals, families, and communities. Journal of interpersonal violence, 23(3), 316-338.

4. Hensley, M. (2006). Empowering parents of multicultural backgrounds. In Funds of knowledge (pp. 143-151). Routledge.

5. Hoffman, D. M. (1996). Culture and self in multicultural education: Reflections on discourse, text, and practice. American educational research journal, 33(3), 545-569.

6. ERIC - Education Resources Information Center. (2019). Ed.gov. https://files.eric.ed.gov/

7. Seider, S., Huguley, J., McCobb, E., Titchner, D., Ward, K., Xu, H., & Zheng, Y. (2023). How Parents in Multiethnic-Racial Families Share Cultural Assets with Their Children. Race and Social Problems. https://doi.org/10.1007/s12552-022-09384-1

8. Breaking Down Barriers and Stereotypes | ATD. (n.d.). Www.td.org. https://www.td.org/atd-blog/breaking-down-barriers-and-stereotypes

9. Rymanowicz, K. (2016, April 22). *The importance of making connections - MSU Extension.* MSU College of Agriculture and Natural Resources. Retrieved June 3, 2023, from https://www.canr.msu.edu/news/the_importance_of_making_connections

10. Solomon, S. (2021, October 29). *5 Ways to Help Multiracial Kids Embrace Every Part of Their Identity - ParentsTogether.* Parents Together. Retrieved June 3, 2023, from https://parents-together.org/5-ways-to-help-multiracial-kids-embrace-every-part-of-their-identity/

CHAPTER 3

1. Parker, J. G., Rubin, K. H., Erath, S. A., Wojslawowicz, J. C., & Buskirk, A. A. (2015). Peer relationships, child development, and adjustment: A developmental psychopathology perspective. Developmental psychopathology: Volume one: Theory and method, 419-493.

2. Fredricks, J. A., & Eccles, J. S. (2006). Is extracurricular participation associated with beneficial outcomes? Concurrent and longitudinal relations. Developmental psychology, 42(4), 698.
3. Tiffany Jana (Author), Michael Baran (Author). Subtle Acts of Exclusion: How to Understand, Identify, and Stop Microaggressions Paperback – March 10, 2020
4. Hall, G. C. N. (2022). Multicultural psychology. Routledge.
5. Scherr, S., Mares, M. L., Bartsch, A., & Goetz, M. (2019). Parents, television, and children's emotional expressions: a cross-cultural multi-level model. Journal of Cross-Cultural Psychology, 50(1), 22-46.

CHAPTER 4

1. Does Anybody Else Look Like Me? (2024). A Parent's Guide to Raising Multiracial Children by Donna Jackson Nakazawa
2. 8 Ways to Show Young Children that Diversity is a Strength | Inclusion Lab. (2017). Brookespublishing.com. https://blog.brookespublishing.com/8-ways-to-show-young-children-that-diversity-is-a-strength/
3. 6 ways to show your child that diversity is a strength. (2021, April 16). St Nicholas Early Education. https://stnicholasmn.org.au/news-1/6-ways-to-show-your-child-that-diversity-is-a-strength#:~:text=Observe%20your%20children%20in%20their
4. 15 Tips for Building Stronger Cross-cultural Relationships. (2019, October 15). Our Saviour's Community Services. https://oscs-mn.org/15-tips-for-building-stronger-cross-cultural-relationship

CHAPTER 5

1. Haque. (2023, June 10). Navigating Cultural Differences in Relationships: Building Bridges, Fostering Understanding. Medium. https://medium.com/@haqueb560/navigating-cultural-differences-in-relationships-building-bridges-fostering-understanding-7a084f572e8f

2. Krumrey, K. (2022). Chapter 7 – Relationships. Openoregon.pressbooks.pub. https://openoregon.pressbooks.pub/comm115/chapter/chapter-7/